ORPHANED
NO MORE

ORPHANED NO MORE

The Boyhood Story
of
Rev. Henry Clay Morrison

Retold by
GARY BEWLEY AND NANCY RICHEY
ILLUSTRATED BY GARY BEWLEY

Acclaim Press
MORLEY, MISSOURI

Acclaim Press
— *Your Next Great Book* —

P.O. Box 238
Morley, MO 63767
(573) 472-9800
www.acclaimpress.com

Book Design: Ron Eifert
Cover Design: Frene Melton

ISBN: 978-1-948901-17-8 | 1-948901-17-X
Library of Congress Control Number: 2019901501

First Printing: 2019
Printed in the United States of America
10 9 8 7 6 5 4 3 2 1

This publication was produced using available information.
The publisher regrets it cannot assume responsibility for errors or omissions.

Contents

There once lived a man named Henry Clay Morrison, one of the greatest evangelists of all time. He preached all over the nation and in many different parts of the world. Additionally, Morrison wrote books, was the publisher and editor of a very popular religious newspaper, served as president of a Christian college and founded a theological seminary. William Jennings Bryan called him "the greatest preacher on the American continent." Morrison did many marvelous things in his service for the Lord, however, some of the most beautiful events of his life are the stories of his youth and the extraordinary way God began using him as a young boy. He was converted at an altar of prayer to a life in the Lord's service.

May God bless everyone in a special way who reads this story, and may each young soul find true heart-felt salvation just like that which was found in the life of our own beloved, Henry Clay Morrison.

Dedicated to Bryson, Andrew and Matthew Jones
and to every beautiful child, everywhere, who we
pray will seek the Lord Jesus Christ to the
salvation of their precious souls. In addition,
this is dedicated to Gary's daughter, Kuristen Jones
and Nancy's son, Shane Marshall.
Lastly, the book is dedicated
to our dearest friend and supporter,
Mr. Gale E. Renner of Batavia, Illinois.

Foreword

Gary's journey with Henry Clay Morrison began around the kitchen table. His dear grandmother infused Morrison with such attributes that these left an indelible mark on his imagination. Fast forward to 2010, and this admiration for Morrison fueled the restoration of Morrison's campmeeting site and this biography.

Many people outside of select religious organizations may never have heard of this remarkable man. Even in his home county of Barren, many had forgotten. It is the purpose and hope of this book to introduce readers to Morrison's life and the One whom he served.

Years of research into Morrison and the local places and people of the area have been put forth. Morrison told his own story in several biographical works, and it is from these that we have quoted freely and from other sources telling Morrison's story. We have focused on his time in Barren County and the events of his life in this area.

We want to gratefully acknowledge WKU Professors Jonathan Jeffrey and Nancy Baird for reading the manuscript and providing very helpful suggestions, thus producing an improved work.

Special thanks to Asbury Theological Seminary archives and Grace Yoder and also, Doug Sikes and Randy Baumgardner of Acclaim Press for their friendship and support.

—Nancy Richey

ORPHANED NO MORE

The Boyhood Story
of
Rev. Henry Clay Morrison

Part 1

The Early Years of Henry Clay Morrison — Dedicated to God and Called to Preach

One Sunday morning in 1857, a young mother named Emily Morrison went to church, leaving her newborn son at home in the care of a trusted friend. She was a good, faithful mother who loved God, the story of Jesus, and the gospel message very much. Emily knew that the way for lost sinners to find salvation and someday go to heaven was to learn about Jesus Christ the Savior, and how he died on the cross for our sins. It was a beautiful story that she learned from ministers who preached the Gospel from the Bible, the true word of God. Emily was very close to God in spirit for she had believed in Jesus and had been saved.

On this particular Sunday morning, Emily prayed a special prayer to God. She asked God to accept her child in service for the Lord. There was a Biblical story that Emily was surely familiar with where a grateful mother named Hannah offered her son Samuel to the Lord in somewhat the same way. Emily left the church rejoicing, telling others of her prayer and how she felt sure God had accepted her son. Somehow she just knew God would some day use her son in a special way.

It is not always easy to understand or explain why some things happen, but not long after this event took place, Emily died, leaving her small boy and his sister without a mother. Perhaps her death was

Emily Morrison and her baby boy, Buddy

somehow necessary for the work God had planned for this young boy who would grow up to be one of the greatest preachers of all time. The young boy's name was Henry Clay Morrison. He was named after an uncle who had the very same name. Now, because there were two Henry Clays in the family, most folks started calling the young boy, Buddy.

After his mother's death, young Buddy and his sister Emma were in the care of their father, James Morrison. James was a businessman and had to earn a living. He decided to leave their home in Bedford, Kentucky and bring the children to where their grandfather lived in rural Barren County, Kentucky, over 100 miles away. The children were supposed to stay for a short time, while their father conducted his business. Barren County was a wonderful place to live. Here, was a loving grandfather, William and grandmother, Francis, and a very special Aunt Lizzie. Lizzie, a sister to their father, James, had no husband and no children, so she became a mother to Buddy and Emma. Buddy's grandparent's home, a rustic, pioneer type cabin, sat on the side of the road that ran between Glasgow and Tompkinsville. It was a nice farm, with barns, orchards and all kinds

Henry Clay and Emma Morrison arriving at their grandfather's home in Barren County, Kentucky.

15

of farm animals. Nearby lay fields to work, run and play in. There were forests, hills and creeks, with wild animals, fish and all types of places to explore. A one-room school sat nearby that the children would one day attend, and the greatest thing of all which would have a deep impact on their lives, the little log country church of Boyd's Creek.

Buddy's father had been gone for quite a while. Buddy, barely two years old when his father left him in Barren County, soon forgot what his father looked like. But, after a time Buddy was told his father was coming for a visit. Buddy wanted to see his father badly. Aunt Lizzie told the children all about their father, where he had

Buddy and Emma

been, all the sights he had seen in his travels, and how he would soon be back to see them and share all of his adventures. This visit was the most important thing in the world to little Buddy and his sister.

A letter arrived that said he would be coming next month. To the excited children, it seemed an eternity, but weeks slowly turned into days, and finally it was the day before his arrival. The children went to bed early so they could arise early, hoping this would bring their father back all the sooner. The next morning, their grandfather hitched up the team and went into Glasgow to bring their father home. The children watched as he drove over the hill out of sight. Before their grandfather could have even had a chance to get to town, some four miles away, they were already eager for his return. The children watched down the roadway all the long day. They could scarcely do or think of anything else. Finally, their hearts grew frantic, worried that something bad might have happened. As the sun was about to set and shadows from the trees stretched long across the pastures, the children were at the point of tears, full of despair and disappointment.

Finally, the wagon came into view. Grandfather sat on the driver's seat and the man at his side wore a silk top hat. The children could not remember how their father looked so they didn't know what to do, or how to react. Was it their father? Aunt Lizzie came out of the cabin and saw the wagon approaching. She told the anxious children, "That's your father." It was just too good to be true. The children took off running, climbed the yard fence and ran down the road to meet him. When their father saw them, he leaped out of the wagon and ran to them. Emma being two years older ran faster and got there first. He caught Emma in his arms and kissed her, then he ran to little Buddy. After many tears of joy, hugs and kisses, their father picked Buddy up, carried him across the yard and into the house. They were all so happy. Their father's visit only lasted about a week, but Buddy made the most of every moment. He rode on his father's back, walked by his side, sat on his knee, went to sleep in his arms by the fire, and slept by his side every night. When it was time for his father to leave, Buddy could hardly stand to let him go. He cried, struggled and begged to go with him, but it just was not possible. His father kissed the children goodbye, once again, leaving them in the good hands of his loving family.

The children's father returns for a visit.

After the short visit, their father traveled south to Mississippi to take a drove of horses and mules to sell. He sold part of the pack, and while in Mississippi, he rented a farm and raised a crop of cotton. This kept him away from the children for about a year. Their father, who was greatly missed, was the subject of much conversation back at home. Finally, they received a letter. It was just one paragraph, but it was so important, everyone in the family seemed to memorize it. It said, "The war is coming on. Mississippi has drawn off from the Union. I am winding up my business and will be coming home as soon as possible." The children had little idea what a war meant, but if it brought their father back home, they saw it as a good thing.

The Civil War to little children could be an exciting time, but also a very scary time. When the war broke out, almost immediately, young men from the area volunteered for both armies, the Northern and the Southern. This was a dark time in our nation's history, when our country was torn apart by disagreement and much anger. The South had tried to secede from the United States, and the North was trying to preserve the union and keep them from leaving. Many battles were fought all across our country and great numbers of men died during the four year struggle. It was a terrible, horrible time.

At home in Glasgow, and in Barren County, men began forming, training, drilling, and preparing for war. Young Buddy even saw soldiers marching and walking along the road in front of his house, and sometimes could see them drilling in the nearby fields. At first Buddy, found it a time of excitement. He and his friends got caught up in the spirit of playing soldier and army. They rode broomstick horses and carried wooden swords. Sometimes, they attacked his grandmother's geese, and sent them scurrying away in fear.

Buddy was now four years old. One day while playing soldier, building up a make believe fort out of chips and sticks of wood, he saw his Uncle Hezekiah, who lived several miles away, gallop up the road. His uncle threw his bridle rein over the fence, and started down the path to the house, pulling a letter out of his pocket as he went. Soon, Buddy heard a lot of weeping in the house, and hurried inside to find out what had happened. Grandfather Morrison was sitting with his head bowed, tears falling to the floor. It was the first time Buddy had ever seen his Grandfather cry. His sister Emma and Aunt Lizzie were crying too. Buddy went to his Aunt and fearfully asked, "What's wrong? Why is everyone crying?" Lizzie took Buddy up in her lap and held him tight for a long while.

Finally, she broke the silence and found the courage to tell him, "Buddy, your father is dead."

Buddy jumped out of her lap, and said, "I know that isn't true. My father can't be dead!"

Poor Buddy was choking with sorrow. He ran from the house and into the barn. Then he ran to the garden, to the orchard, and all around the old homestead. He did not know what he was looking for, but he was searching for something. In time, Buddy realized he was searching for something he would never find. His father was gone. He would never see him again in this world. All Buddy could do now was to cling to the memory of his father and hold dear the remembrance of that wonderful visit. Buddy would often dream and think, "Maybe it was a mistake, and someday he might come riding up the road just as he had done before." But finally, that dream vanished, and sadly, he accepted the fact that he was a boy without a mother and a father. He was now an orphan. But this great loss drew Buddy and his sister all the more closer to their grandparents and their wonderful Aunt Lizzie. Still, Buddy often thought about his father as he grew up. Later, when he was old enough to attend the Bald Knob School, he sometimes changed the words to poems and verses he learned, just to pacify his own loss and grief.

One poem he changed went like this:

"Of all the beautiful pictures that hang on memory's wall, there is one of a dim old forest that seemeth the brightest of all."

After reading the verse, Buddy searched his heart, and then rewrote it to suit himself:

"Of all the precious pictures that hang on memory's wall, there is one of the open arms of my father that seemeth the brightest of all."

Although Buddy and his sister could never forget the sadness associated with their father's death, the immediate events of the Civil War drew the children's attention and imagination. Buddy continued to see the soldiers drilling and marching. At first, many of the young men didn't even have uniforms and guns, but eventually Buddy witnessed a group of soldiers marching along the road shooting their rifles into the trees, jubilant over a small victory in capturing some young men at a nearby training camp, named "Camp Underwood." Buddy was curious but fearful. He ran into the house and went upstairs. There was a small window in the front of the house just large enough that he could poke his little face through and see the soldiers passing by. To Buddy, all the shots being fired meant that there was battle and war.

Buddy's grandfather had a large apple orchard, and much of the fruit was now ripe. While Buddy was looking out the window one day, a number of soldiers turned off the road, climbed the fence, and entered the apple orchard. Buddy thought they must be coming in to hurt him and all his family. He screamed with all he had, giving away his hiding place. His family immediately rushed in and was soon able to calm him, assuring him that no one was going to hurt him, and that all the soldiers wanted were some apples.

On another occasion, an old army soldier actually came into their house. He sat down in their front room, and talked with his grandmother. Buddy was so scared by the soldier's presence that he ran out the back door and hid between two outside chimneys. It wasn't long before a superior officer arrived looking for the old soldier. When the soldier saw the officer, he ran out the back door also, and ran right to the spot where Buddy was hiding. This scared poor Buddy to death, again causing the young boy to scream and run for his life. Buddy's grandfather was coming home from a neighbor's house when he saw the officer ride up and dismount. He saw the soldier running, then heard Buddy scream. He became very alarmed and ran to the house to see what was happening. The old soldier was running through the orchard, his superior officer was running after him, and Grandfather was running after Buddy. It was an exciting afternoon! After everything was understood, they all had a great laugh about it, but Buddy never forgot the fear that the old soldier had brought into his home.

Buddy at the "Bald Knob" School near his home.

Very soon the family had to face another soldier. He came into the house and demanded Buddy's grandmother cook a chicken. This time when Buddy began to cry, the soldier actually caught him by the arm and gave him a shake and said, "If you cry another whimper, I'll jerk the last bit of hide off of you in a minute." Buddy did not cry another whimper! He was frightened voiceless. Buddy's grandmother prepared the chicken, and as the soldier sat eating it, Grandfather went outside and met some soldiers coming down the road, and demanded they remove the soldier from his home. Soon the mean, hungry soldier was gone.

Despite the constant threat of battles looming about, young Buddy was growing up, and much more courageous. His fears seemed to leave him. Once officers made camp on a hillside that was part of his grandfather's farm, and after they had left, he and Aunt Lizzie went up to their camp to investigate. There were campfires left burning and in some places cooking utensils were left lying about the fires. There was a great clump of lilac bushes in the back of his grandfather's garden, and Buddy would later sit on the yard fence and offer them to the soldiers as they passed by. Buddy found most soldiers, both of the North and South, very courteous and kind. Often times, they would stop and eat much needed food, and they

Buddy making friends with the passing soldiers.

generally paid for it. Buddy soon learned not to be afraid and made friends with many of the soldiers.

Times did grow hard during the war years. Sometimes food items and luxuries became scarce and clothing material very costly. For a time, clothing for boys of the ages of six or seven consisted of a garment that was more like a long robe. It had a button at the neck with plenty of sleeve room, slits on the sides which gave room to run and play, and came down below the knees. Buddy wore a garment like this for some time. The advantage of such an outfit was it could be worn for sleeping as well. All he had to do to prepare for bed was to wash his feet. In the morning, Buddy found himself already dressed, and with a little washing, was set and ready to enjoy the day. He saved his best clothes for special days, such as church time, and of course, more clothes were added for the winter months.

Buddy heard the older folks talk about the sorrows of the war. They spoke of and discussed terrible battles. There was news of young men from the neighborhood who were killed in the war, never to return. They spoke of how the war divided families by the taking of different sides in the conflict, and frequently even brothers of the same family could be found fighting against each other in battle. It was a most terrible time.

All the talk of war generated family stories, too. Young Buddy heard stories of how his great-great-grandfather, Andrew Morrison, came from northern Ireland to America, in time to participate in the Revolutionary War. This was the war against British rule, when our country fought to become a nation. "Your great-great-grandfather," Buddy was told, "was killed at the Battle of Brandywine for his adopted homeland." This battle was fought in September 1777 near Philadelphia, Pennsylvania. Buddy also had a great-grandfather on his mother's side who had fought in the War of 1812. His name was Francis Scott. Then Buddy learned of his great-grandfather, John Organ Morrison, who came from Virginia to Kentucky in 1793. He settled in Barren County and bought one hundred acres on the south side of Boyd's Creek. This was the very land Buddy was now living on, having been passed down to his grandfather. His great-grandfather built the first brick home in the area, and it was still standing. It had been handed down to his

The Hammer House

grandfather's sister, Mary Jane Morrison. She married Peter Emory Hammer, so the old Morrison home, soon became known as the Hammer house.

Buddy visited the Hammer house sometimes, and there he saw a large painted portrait of his great-grandfather, an old time Virginia gentleman who wore his hair plaited hanging down his back and tied with a ribbon. This was the style of the day. John O. Morrison had been an officer in the hometown militia, and Buddy saw and held his old sword that had been kept by the family, long after his death. Not far from his great-grandfather's old home was the family cemetery. Here Buddy could walk among the old stones and think of his ancestors buried there. His great-great-grandmother, Margaret (Burdette) Morrison was born on July 4, 1776, the very day that the Declaration of Independence was signed. Buddy took a lot of pride in the fact that even the highway he lived on, which ran from Glasgow to Tompkinsville was popularly known as the "Morrison Road." This no doubt occurred because his great-grandfather owned a good amount of the land adjacent to the road, and had the job of maintaining a large portion of it. All this was special to Buddy.

Buddy, with the portrait and sword of his great-grandfather, John O. Morrison.

As Buddy grew up, he never forgot he was an orphan, but along with the thoughts of his loss, he recognized he had been given many blessings. What a wonderful family he had. He adored his big sister, he loved his Aunt Lizzie just like a mother, and then there were his wonderful grandparents. Buddy enjoyed seeing his grandfather when he got all dressed up to go to town, or to church. Grandfather wore a silk, stovepipe hat and a broadcloth Prince Albert coat. Buddy thought he was the handsomest man anywhere. His grandfather and his grandmother had a wonderful relationship. When he addressed her, he would bow his head and extend his hands in courtesy as if she were a princess. There was no arguing or cruel talk, only a beautiful love, reverence and affection between them that brought a spirit of order and quietness into the home.

Other than during the lean years of the Civil War, the family generally had plenty. They were not rich with money, but they had all they needed for a good home life. They made their living from the soil, raised their wheat and had abundance of vegetables and fruits. They butchered their meat and had ham, beef and mutton. When relatives visited there was always good meals, tender affection and genuine happiness.

Alongside what the Morrisons raised, wild game was also available. During the war years, there was very little hunting for most people didn't like hearing the sound of a gun being fired. Game increased wonderfully and the forests in the area overflowed with squirrels, coons and opossums. The forest was also thick with berries and nuts. The streams were filled with fish, and it was easy with proper traps to catch rabbits and quail. Buddy learned to use these traps and kept the family well supplied with food. His grandfather even gave him a gun. It was a small muzzle-loading shotgun, and it was an unusually fine fowling piece. Buddy also learned to trap certain animals like coons and sell their hides. Once, he sold the hide of a big coon for twenty-five cents, a large amount of money for a young boy.

Buddy had many friends, and they loved to spend Saturday afternoons together. Most every boy his age had morning chores to do. The boys would work hard to get them all done, so they could be free for an afternoon of enjoyment. If someone was not finished, the other boys generally came over and helped out. They worked to thin and hoe out the corn. They planted crops or whatever had to be done to set everyone free for a delightful Saturday afternoon. And then, they were away into the woods or down by the creek. There was sport and freedom; they generally went home with fish, game, nuts or wild grapes for their families.

The boys lived in an area where there were two major denominations. There was a Baptist church and a Methodist church. Most everyone's family belonged to or attended one of these two churches. It was a peaceful time when almost everyone in the community worshipped the Lord, and lived among each other with Christian fellowship and love. The big log Baptist church, called Siloam, sat on a hill about half a mile from Boyd's Creek. The Methodist church, called Boyd's Creek Meetinghouse, stood near the creek bank.

Each year, both congregations conducted a revival, and the pastors of these churches united and held union meetings. The people who were saved had an opportunity to join whichever church they desired. The two ministers stood up in the front of the church, and the new converts made their choice known by taking the minister's hand.

When Buddy went to church, he heard the ministers preach about many things. There were sermons about the evils of sin and how its wickedness separated us from God and all that is good and righteous. They also preached about Jesus, who had suffered upon a cross, shedding His innocent blood for our sins. They preached about the danger of rebellion against God, of violating His law and

Boyd's Creek Meetinghouse

28

rejecting His mercy. There was a lot of preaching about the Judgment Day and about a great separation that would take place, the saved going to heaven and the lost entering into eternal torment in a terrible place called Hell. Buddy and his friends were often frightened when they heard the stories about Hell, and feared doing anything wrong that would provoke or bring displeasure to God. Buddy understood the word of God was a serious and important thing.

It was very common for the men of the church, especially the elders of the congregation to bow near the front pulpit area of the church and pray. The minister usually called upon one particular individual to lead the prayer, but almost everyone joined in unison. In these prayers, they praised and thanked God, and asked favors and blessings upon their homes, their churches, their families and friends. Also, of greater importance was the prayer for the conviction of sinners, that they too might come to an altar of prayer and seek the mercy of God through Jesus Christ, God's son. These union prayers often went on for quite some time and almost everyone prayed aloud. Then gradually, one by one, they would begin to fade away, till only the designated leader would be left to conclude and close the prayer. Then, slowly and quietly all rose and returned to their seats, to sing another hymn and await the sermon from the preacher. At the close of most services, an invitation was given, welcoming and urging those without Christ to come to the altar of prayer. Most people called this particular place, located near the foot of the pulpit, a mourner's bench. Upon this bench, the lost would pray, plead and commonly cry out for God's mercy. The length of time upon the altar for some seekers could be quite brief, while others might spend several nights, or even weeks upon their knees. In some instances, the weary sinner might even give up for a time and return to the congregation in much sorrow and distress, pondering what human or worldly waywardness was preventing their conversion. Occasionally, the revival meetings would close, leaving some lost sinners still at the altar.

Away from church, many of those who were under conviction spent a lot of time in silence, praying in the woods, out in a barn or maybe in some hidden place in their field. After a time,

Buddy heard stories in church about how these people had been saved. There was always much excitement among the congregation when this happened. The converts gave joyous testimonies of all the comfort and happiness they felt when they got saved. Many even went about the neighborhood witnessing about what the Lord had done for them.

The Lord's Day, Sunday, was very important to everyone. It was considered holy, not only to those who went to church, but it seemed so to everyone throughout the whole community. They attended church, they rested, maybe they visited other family members, but no one did any work, other than that which was absolutely necessary. This work included feeding and caring for livestock and milking cows. In the cooler months, Buddy's task of bringing in wood had to be done early on Saturday evening in preparation for a quiet Sunday. Buddy had been in church all his life, so it seemed only natural that he would feel some guilt and conviction for anything he might do that he felt would be unpleasing to God. Sometimes on Sunday, he might feel tempted to go off with some of his friends. In the light of day, when everything seemed sunny and so well, he might be tempted to go fishing or hunting. But when evening came, and darkness set in, he would not dare bring his catches home, for with this darkness also came great guilt and fear. Buddy's conviction became so intense that he could not stay in bed. Buddy often ran to the arms of his Aunt Lizzie, who sat up with him and held him providing some amount of comfort. Aunt Lizzie would say "The child is not well; he is nervous." But Buddy knew that he was suffering from a profound sense of sin and guilt.

When Buddy was twelve years old, a young minister named Reverend James Phillips was sent to his church and other neighboring churches to hold revivals. Reverend Phillips was tall and handsome, beaming with the grace of God and full of love for everyone. He led the song services with a melodious voice. He rode a horse and traveled all around the community getting acquainted with everyone. He was loved by all and became everyone's "Brother Phillips." Brother Phillips held revivals in all the area Methodist churches starting in the fall of 1870. Many people were saved and joined these

Young Buddy Morrison and his Aunt Lizzie

churches. When he came to Buddy's church, Boyd's Creek, people crowded in to hear him, among these were Buddy's sister, Emma and many schoolmates and friends. His sister went to the altar for prayer and Buddy wanted to go too. But, being small for his age and very timid, he felt others would be convinced he was not old enough to understand the truth about the gospel. The likely reason that Buddy felt this way had much to do with a practice that went on within the church. The Christians would go out into the audience and invite sinners to the mourner's bench. They wept over them, instructed them and did all they could to lead them to Christ and salvation. Buddy sat near the front, just hoping and praying someone would speak to him and ask him to come and pray. During one service, he sat and wept, but no one seemed to take any notice of him. Buddy was very distraught and grieved about his condition. Then the meeting was over. Others got saved, but he did not. He was quite disappointed and emotionally upset.

When spring arrived, Buddy plowed corn in the fields of his grandfather's farm. While working, Buddy found himself full of bitterness about his condition. Others about his age had gotten saved, but he was still lost. He reasoned to himself:

"No one cares about you. No one asked you to the altar to pray. You are young, an orphan boy; you have no parents, no money and nobody cares one bit about you. Time and time again, you went up and sat at the front of the church, just hoping that someone would care enough to come over to speak to you, but no one cared and no one came."

Then Buddy began to reason that he would just get even. He decided he would just show them, by being rebellious. "I'll show them. I will swear; I'll drink whiskey; I'll carry a pistol; I'll fight and be so bad that these people will regret that they didn't care enough to try and get me saved when I was a boy."

Instead of enjoying the wonderful Spring day and praying to the Lord for salvation, Buddy allowed himself to be filled with anger and resentment. This bitterness went on for quite some time and

Buddy contemplates his dilemma as he plows the field.

only seemed to deepen. He was able to hide this anger from his family, but when he was alone, he let it out. Buddy used profanity. He cursed the stock and all the animals. If the plow did not run just right to suit him, he cursed the plow. Anything that did not please him or aroused his anger brought bad words. When Buddy acted this way and used this profanity, it often scared him within. But then, he would convince himself that was just the way it was going to have to be, for he was a nobody. He was just an orphan, unwanted and uncared for by those in the community. He felt he could never be of any use to the church and was not good enough to be a part of it anyway.

In the midst of all this anger and despair, there remained several important glimmers of hope that would prove triumphant in bringing young Buddy back to good conduct. First, there was his family who loved him and expected the best from him. But it seemed, the greatest influence that the Lord sent into the path of the misguided boy was the Reverend James Phillips. When the stalwart Buddy went about his way, convinced and settled firmly into his new life of rebellion, the mere sight of Brother Phillips riding by challenged his heart and feelings of waywardness. To young Buddy, despite his dim view concerning the uncaring nature of the church members toward his condition, he still considered Brother Phillips a great man. Something inside him spoke plainly that Brother Phillips was a true man of God. Despite all the anger that Buddy focused toward the church, he loved and greatly admired Brother Phillips. "He's the best man I ever saw," Buddy thought. "I sure would like to be like him and to have what he has got." But then, he would try to make himself angry at Brother Phillips by his selfish reasoning: "Brother Phillips would go out and talk to others and invite them to the altar, but he never invited me." The victory over this embedded anger of his soul would finally and forever be dissolved by his great admiration for Brother Phillips. Oh, what a splendid thrill would run through him when Phillips would say, "Bud, I am glad to see you at church." Buddy was so excited with this attention afforded him by this Godly man, that he would hurry home and with much pride, joy and enormous pleasure, tell his Aunt Lizzie, "Brother Phillips said that he was glad to see me today."

In the few remaining times that year that Brother Phillips preached in the nearby community, Buddy always made plans to attend. He finally resolved within himself, "Maybe Brother Phillips will come back on the circuit next year and if he holds a revival at Boyd's Creek Meetinghouse, I will go to the mourner's bench and seek salvation, whether anyone asks me or not." Buddy spent the following year in much prayer, asking forgiveness for all his bad conduct and praying to God for Brother Phillips' return. Buddy vowed to God, "If you will let him come back, I will seek salvation no matter what."

In the fall of the following year, Buddy was digging potatoes in a patch near the road. A member of the Methodist Church rode by and Buddy called to him, "Have you heard from the conference? Who is going to be our circuit rider?" He said, "The same man as last year, Brother Phillips." Conviction shot through Buddy like an arrow. He remembered his sacred vow. Buddy knew he had to do all the things that he had promised to himself and especially to God. If he did not, he believed the Lord would be finished with him for good and he would be forever lost.

When revival time came around, Buddy found himself involved in a school contest where the student with the highest mark received a prize. His eagerness to win that prize kept him away from the mourner's bench for several nights. When heavy rains kept his closest competitor, a little girl named Louisa Mansfield away from school, Buddy won the contest. The prize was seventy-five cents. To a young boy of thirteen, this newly acquired financial reward made him feel quite prosperous and most enterprising. However, it was soon evident that the pride and pleasure he afforded to himself was only to be enjoyed for a brief moment. It soon began to fade and dim. Buddy suddenly realized he was not so rich and secure in things that mattered most.

On Thursday at noon, the school closed its doors for the Christmas holiday and Buddy turned all his attention to the revival. He had made up his mind to go forward for prayer that night. He went up and sat at the end of the third bench, hoping someone would come to him, but no one came. An invitation was soon made for those who were lost and without Christ to come to an altar of prayer. Buddy's heart was stirring madly. Every fiber of his body seemed oddly alive and burning with a raging fire, needing and wanting to go forward. Buddy realized he had reached the very moment in time that had been the subject of his many prayers and hopes. For an entire year, he had longed for this opportunity. But now a weakness had come upon him and doubts began to arise. Could he go down in front of everyone and pray? Would he really get saved? What would people think? He felt as though his feet were now riveted to the floor. Uncertain at the time as to whether it was strong conviction that moved him or his vow to the Lord, he finally resolved within himself enough strength to break free and almost ran to the place of prayer.

Buddy was not successful in finding salvation his first night on the altar, but something wonderful had happened. The fear, fright and worry that had once plagued him were now gone. Buddy no longer worried about what people thought or if someone would come and invite him to pray. The Spirit of the Lord was now upon him and he was determined to seek Jesus and find salvation at any cost.

By church time the next morning, Buddy eagerly entered the door, hastened up the aisle and knelt at the altar before the preacher

Buddy at an altar of prayer while Rev. James Phillips conducts the service.

could even began his text. He cried to the Lord for mercy. He was not ashamed for people to see or hear him. Buddy promised the Lord many things he would do for Him if He would save him. Although Buddy was as sincere as he thought he could be, he was still not successful. He went back to the altar Friday night, Saturday morning and again Saturday night. In between these services, he was almost constantly in prayer and he felt he was sinking deeper and deeper into darkness. Buddy was so determined. He knew he must be saved and would not give up. Sunday morning, he went to church very early before others arrived. He went straight to the altar, fell upon his knees and commenced praying.

Buddy stayed at the altar until the church was full and throughout the service. Others came to the altar and many were converted. There was rejoicing. Finally, Buddy alone remained, the only one not saved. He was so distraught. His sister Emma kneeled and prayed at his side, while Brother Phillips knelt on the other side, praying and encouraging him to continue and just trust the Lord. Buddy prayed on and on until finally the church emptied. Brother Phillips said, "We shall have to go, but keep on seeking the Lord and you are sure to find salvation.

Buddy went home once again with a heavy heart. Worn out with grief, he wondered if he would ever get saved. He found his tears had stopped flowing and he was startled to find his great burden of heart seemed to go away. Buddy was afraid God's drawing Spirit had left him.

Clouds came up in the evening and it looked as if it would rain. It was very dark and gloomy. Buddy's grandfather told him, "Son, it looks as if it would rain tonight and if it does you mustn't go to church. You have been out many nights of late, and if you get wet, you will be sick." Buddy was so upset. He felt as if he would die if he could not go to church this night. He felt he would be lost forever.

Buddy went to a secret place of prayer, the chimney corner, and there he prayed earnestly to God that it might not rain. Buddy watched the clouds with great concern, often growing frantic as the skies grew darker and darker. Three times he went to this secret place of prayer, begging the Lord to drive the dark clouds from the sky and just as the sun was going down, the clouds lifted and the Lord poured out a great flood of light. Buddy was so happy, so thankful and greatly encouraged. He somehow just knew that the Lord had heard him and had heeded his heart's desire.

"Surely, if the Lord would answer this prayer," Buddy reasoned, "Surely, He will answer my prayer to save me." Buddy now ran to his grandfather and respectfully reported, "Grandfather, I don't think it is going to rain." Buddy was elated when he was given permission

"Prayer for Fair Weather" oil on canvas, 16" x 20" (2015) by Gary Bewley

to go to church and was off in great haste. He feared a change in the weather conditions might result in a change of his grandfather's decision.

By now it was getting a little late. Buddy quickly bridled his pony and galloped all the way to the church about a mile and a half away. When he arrived, the church was full and the service had already begun. Buddy found there was no room at the mourner's bench; it was full of seekers. So he knelt down at the front bench in the "amen corner," up next to the wall and commenced to pray. Buddy did not really hear the sermon, being so occupied with his own prayer. After the sermon concluded, the people sang and many church members came around to encourage and help the seekers at the altar.

Someone came up to Buddy with news that Joe Mansfield had just found peace. "Take courage, the Lord will save you too," they said. Instead of feeling happy or encouraged, it seemed to drive young Buddy into deeper despair. To think that the Lord had been so close as to save Joe Mansfield and not save him was just too hard to bear.

At this moment, everything seemed so hopeless. But just then, something happened. Suddenly the Spirit of God revealed so much to Buddy. He saw and understood things as he never had before. God made Buddy to understand how sinful his life had been. The Lord showed him the self-righteousness he brought with him to the altar. He showed him how he had tried to buy salvation by promising the Lord to do many things. He showed him how many times he had rejected Christ. Up to this time Buddy thought and feared that he was lost, but now he knew he was lost. Buddy pushed back from the bench and lay face down upon the floor. It seemed to him as though he was sinking lower and lower. Buddy was wailing aloud in such agony and despair, that an old gentleman came up to him and looked down mercifully upon his complicated plight. It was Peter Emory Hammer, the man who had married his great-aunt, Mary Jane Morrison. He was a good man and a deacon in the Baptist Church. Mr. Hammer lifted Buddy off the floor, took him in his arms and held him in his bosom. He had a very heavy beard, but he pressed his mouth through his mustache against Buddy's ear and whispered, "Buddy, God is not mad at you."

That shot through him a ray of hope. Buddy replied, "Sir? Sir? Sir?" He wanted his uncle to repeat those words. Mr. Hammer stayed silent for a time, but finally pressed his lips near Buddy's ear and said, "Buddy, God loves you." What a thrill this gave Buddy and again he desired to hear those beautiful words, saying, "Sir? Sir? Sir?" Mr. Hammer held Buddy tightly in his big arms and again pressed his lips to his ear and whispered, "Buddy, God so loved you that He gave His only son to die for you." Something inside of Buddy said, "That is so."

Almost immediately something happened in his heart. His great burden just went away and the joy of forgiveness went through him. He leaped to his feet praising the Lord. He felt as though he would burst with great happiness and joy. A friend, Mike Smith, was sitting on the steps of the pulpit in front of him. Buddy caught him about the neck and hugged him with all his might. Buddy jumped into the pulpit area and ran across shaking hands with everyone in the little choir. He then faced all the people and began to exhort them to come to Christ. Buddy saw his schoolteacher halfway down the aisle looking at him. Buddy ran out of the pulpit area and ran down the aisle, embraced him and wept. Buddy begged him to give his life to Christ. Everyone looked so beautiful to Buddy and his heart was aglow with love. Buddy had been saved. He was born again and filled with the wonderful Holy Spirit of God. Now he knew the Lord and he knew he had a heavenly Father.

Buddy knew he was an orphan no more.

Buddy's Conversion at Boyd's Creek Methodist Church

At the close of the revival, Buddy chose to join the Methodist Church. He was excited in the joy of his new-found relationship with the Lord, and began to work on His behalf anyway he could. Buddy was baptized in Boyd's Creek. Then he and many of his friends, especially those who had been converted during the same revival, started a weekly prayer meeting in the old log church and had gracious times praying and singing together. Buddy's heart burned with joy, when at the end of the day he mounted his pony and galloped away to those prayer meetings. They truly loved each other and the Lord with all their hearts.

Buddy soon felt the call to preach, and it was talked about throughout the neighborhood that Bud Morrison was going to be a preacher. Buddy continued to gather with his friends for prayer meetings, and when revivals were held at Temple Hill or Old Bethel Church, he and his friend, Mike Smith mounted their horses and attended these services. Together they took a seat on the front bench and often wept and rejoiced while the preacher preached. As soon as the sermon ended and the invitation was given, Mike would go down one aisle, and Buddy went down the other, to beseech the lost, especially the young boys to come to the mourner's bench. The people often said to each other, "Things will move now. Mike Smith and Bud Morrison's come."

The Lord blessed their efforts very much, and many neighborhood boys prayed through to victory finding Christ as their conscious Savior.

One of the severest tests of Buddy's early Christian life came when he felt strongly impressed to erect a family altar in his adopted home. Buddy's grandfather never led the family in any type of united prayer, and this began to weigh heavily upon Buddy's mind. Buddy felt the Spirit of God was instructing him to do something about this matter. It was a great struggle for him, and he prayed much about it in secret. But for Buddy, it just seemed impossible. Not only would he have to face his own family concerning this, but he realized he would have to perform this task before others who frequented their home.

Visitors and travelers often stopped in, and sometimes neighboring children came home with them from school to spend the

Buddy conducts a worship service in his family home.

night. And then there was an uncle who would come from time to time and spend as much as a week with them in the home. Buddy just felt he could not do this in front of him and others. To ease his way and mind, Buddy kneeled down close to his grandfather at night and prayed, but the Spirit would just not compromise. Buddy felt the Spirit telling him to read the scriptures and pray aloud with all the family every night before retiring.

As time went by, he became desperate. He felt any prayers toward relieving him of this duty only resulted in deteriorating peace and a weakening faith. After much struggling with his doubts and fears, he finally resolved that he must try. Buddy got the big leatherbound Bible in his home, and spent much time reading the scriptures. Finally, he selected a short Psalm and placed a mark in the book so he could find it easily in case he found the strength and determination to proceed.

After dark, Buddy went out in the yard to a fence corner to pray. He walked up and down along the fence, praying first here, and then, there, in this corner, and in that fence corner. It seemed to him his soul's only peace depended upon obeying the Lord this very night. With renewed strength Buddy went in, set a lamp on a little table, took down the Bible and had it in hand. Buddy looked so troubled that his grandfather became a bit uneasy about his condition. His grandfather said, "Son, you have read your Bible enough for today; it is making you nervous. You had better put it up and go to bed."

Buddy replied, "I would like to read one Psalm." "Very well," he said. Buddy began to read. He read with a trembling voice. When he concluded the Psalm, he closed the book and said, "Let us pray." The family was surprised and caught off guard, but they all went down on their knees. Buddy led in prayer. He prayed. He wept. He praised the Lord, and the Lord gave him a wonderful blessing. He had obeyed the Spirit of God and came up off his knees with a victory over his fears and a victory over Satan.

The very next evening, two of his cousins came home with him after school to spend the night. After supper, Buddy again went to his secret place in the yard to pray for strength for the more public service he would soon hold at the family fireside. Buddy faithfully conducted another service of scripture reading, family worship and prayer. From this time forward, Buddy committed himself to these nightly services. Frequently travelers stopped for a night's lodging and after supper, they all sat around the fire. Buddy's Grandfather would say, "Your bedroom for the night is upstairs, but my little grandson always has prayers with us. If you wish you can remain for prayers." The visitors would always remain.

Buddy soon realized all the fears and worries he had concerning obeying the Lord in this matter were unfounded. Instead, he found wonderful joy in serving the Lord. Word spread around the community about the faithfulness of young Bud Morrison in the work of the Lord. He was often called upon in revival meetings, and regular services to lead the congregation in prayer. Buddy grew in grace and always received a blessing from taking part in public worship and service.

Buddy's mother, who died when he was two, had been previously married to Elijah English before marrying Buddy's father. From this first marriage she had four children. Three children lived to adulthood, Robert English, Thomas "Tom" English and Fannie

(English) Meyer. When she died, Buddy's father took the English children to live with their mother's family in Boyle County, Kentucky, near Danville. Because of the great distance between them, and Thomas English's four-year enlistment in the Civil War, Buddy and his sister Emma had no contact with them. A few years after the war ended, and his half-brother had become successful in business, he said to his sister, Fannie, "We ought to hunt those Morrison children. We do not know whether they are living or dead." He began writing letters, located them and wrote that he was coming to visit. Buddy was now sixteen years old.

One evening while coming home from school, Buddy saw a large horse and a handsome buggy standing in the yard. When he got nearer, he could hear crying in the house. Buddy realized that his half-brother and half-sister had come to visit. He was greatly embarrassed. He was barefoot, pants rolled up and his pants were held up by a pair of suspenders made out of old bed ticking. Although he was dressed in the fashion of the community among boys of his age, he wished he could somehow get to his Sunday clothes that were upstairs in the home. To get them, he would have to go into the

Buddy is embarrassed to meet his brother and sister.

44

house where the company waited. Aunt Lizzie came out with tears in her eyes and said, "Your brother and sister have come to see you. Come in the house."

Buddy was greatly embarrassed and did not want to go in. Aunt Lizzie insisted, and began pulling him in. Buddy resisted and pulled against her, but somehow she managed to pull harder and pulled Buddy right in the house. There sat his older, handsome brother and a sister that he had not seen since he was a baby. Emma was there in the midst of them and they were all crying, laughing and embracing each other. Buddy immediately dove into the bunch. He went down on his knees, where he received kisses, hugs and great love. Buddy's embarrassment wore quickly away and he fell in love with his new found relatives. That very night, Tom said, "Brother Henry, we have been separated ever since mother died and I feel we ought not to be separated anymore." To which Buddy answered, "Brother Tom, that is exactly the way I feel." Buddy was so excited; he now had a new brother and sister.

Tom begged Aunt Lizzie to let Buddy and Emma go with them, convincing her that they could care for them better than she could. Buddy was now seventeen, his grandparents had passed away, and many things had changed. Sadly, Aunt Lizzie agreed and consented to let them go. They went into Glasgow and bought goods, and were all busy getting Emma ready to go back with them. She was to go to a female college, the Ewing Institute in Perryville. It was agreed that Buddy was to remain with Aunt Lizzie until the crops were gathered and then he would come live with his brother. Finally, after the harvest, Buddy mounted his pony and rode away from Barren County to the Bluegrass region. He was arrayed in a nice store-bought suit and all his possessions were placed in a pair of saddlebags. It took three days going from Glasgow to Perryville. Aunt Lizzie was afraid for him to make the trip alone and asked a neighbor with a horse to ride with him, a Mr. Ellis who had a sister living in Harrodsburg. Sam Stout also went with them to visit some relatives he had in the area.

This was the first time Buddy had ever been any distance from his grandfather's home. Buddy found a new and interesting world on that three-day trip. They spent the first night in Greensburg, and the second night in Lebanon, Kentucky. On the third afternoon, they rode into Perryville and inquired the way to the home of Mr. John Meyer, the husband of his half-sister. They rode out of town a couple of miles and found their house. It was all a new and strange, yet delightful fresh start in life. Buddy also attended Ewing Institute when enrollment opened for young men, and he did farm work. Often, his brother took him into Danville to meet many influential people such as bankers, lawyers and businessmen. The people Buddy enjoyed meeting the most were Reverend Thomas F. Taliaferro, and his wife, Mary. Soon after coming to Perryville, Brother Taliaferro became the pastor at Perryville Methodist Church and took a keen interest in young Buddy. He and his wife became like a father and mother to him. Rev. Taliaferro soon asked Buddy to assist him in many of the services. This greatly pleased Buddy and the old time glow of Godly love was renewed in his heart. Buddy soon revealed to his pastor, the call he felt from the Lord to preach the gospel.

Brother Taliaferro remained as pastor for three years and insisted that Buddy be licensed to preach before he left the charge at Perryville. He wanted Buddy to come with him to his next appointment, to make his home Buddy's home, and to preach on his circuit and help in meetings. He also assisted the young man with his studies. All these matters were confidential between Buddy and Brother and Sister Taliaferro.

Buddy's brother, Tom, had a very fine horse and a handsome, expensive buggy. One particular Sunday morning, he rode with him into Perryville to attend services at the Methodist Church where they were both members. Before pronouncing the benediction, Brother Taliaferro said, "I desire all the members of the church to remain for a short business meeting after the benediction." When they were seated, he said, "I want you by vote to recommend Henry Morrison to the quarterly conference to be licensed as a local preacher." They took the vote and everyone present but one voted for this recommendation. The dissenting vote, surprisingly, was Buddy's own brother.

Tom was so mad. After the service, he stomped out of the church and leaped into his buggy. Buddy followed him out and before he could get seated, Tom tapped the horse and out they went, barely missing the gatepost. They travelled up the pike at full speed, Tom frequently tapping the horse with the whip. He said, "You and

Rev. Thomas F. Taliaferro

Taliaferro have taken snap judgment on me. I didn't know you were going to get a license to preach. You can't preach. If there is anybody that I am not interested in, it is a one horse Methodist preacher dragging a woman and children around the country at the point of starvation. We have one scrub preacher among our kinfolks and that's enough. I stand in with the congressmen of this district and could have gotten you into West Point and made an Army officer

Tom dashes away from the church in a fit of rage.

out of you; or, I could have put you in with Dr. Meyer and made a physician out of you. You could have been somebody of whom we would feel proud."

Throughout Tom's lecture and hurtful tirade, Buddy was crying bitterly. Finally, Buddy found the resolve to reply, "But Tom, you see the Lord has called me to preach." To which his brother answered, "He must be hard up for material!" While Tom continued in his rampage, tapping the horse with severity, gravel flying back against the buggy under his rapidly moving feet, Buddy kept saying in his heart, "Lord please help me! I am going to preach."

At the next quarterly conference, in the summer of 1878, Henry Clay Morrison was licensed to preach the gospel. The name of Buddy Morrison was soon forgotten, but all the country would one day know the name Reverend Henry Clay Morrison. No one, not even his own brother, could have possibly predicted or have known the great way in which the Lord would use Henry Clay Morrison. He never sought fame or attention, but it came his way naturally as masses of people were drawn to his preaching, his writing, and his ministry. His first sermons were failures, at least in the eyes of man. But through faith, prayer and continual devotion to God, he became one of the most powerful and respected ministers in America.

No one loved the Lord any more than Henry Clay Morrison. No one worked harder or was more dedicated to the work of spreading the Gospel message. No one encouraged Christians more to be holy, to be more righteous, and to seek out the will of the Lord through His Spirit in every aspect of their lives. From the moment Morrison was saved at the meetinghouse at Boyd's Creek, to the day he died at the age of eighty-five while conducting revival services in Elizabethton, Tennessee, he devoted himself fully to the service of the Lord.

Author Bessie G. Olsen wrote, "There are millions of souls saved today because of his faithful preaching and working—directly and indirectly." Author George W. Ridout said, "Dr. Morrison was a prince among the Holiness evangelists of his age." Nebraska Senator, and three-time Presidential candidate, William Jennings Bryan, said, "I regard Henry Clay Morrison the greatest pulpit orator on the American Continent."

Morrison wrote how the events of his early life influenced him and prepared him for all the work that lay ahead. In wayward times, when he felt tempted to give into sin and would pull away from God, he told of how the Lord's gracious Spirit brought vividly to his mind, the memory of the old leather back Bible, the little table and the lamp where he used to pray morning and night. The memory of the blessings, peace and happiness he had received there came rushing in upon him and chased his temptation away.

Morrison never forgot the special night the Lord saved his soul. He would always recall the scenes of that night, the songs they sang and the way they sounded. He could hear the voice of Brother Phillips ringing in his mind and the comforting words of the great gospel message. He could always recall the shining, smiling faces filled with the love of God when he arose a new creature, born again into God's glorious kingdom. He would never forget the marvelous love that fell from heaven that night right into his heart.

Morrison often pondered the question, "What might have been the result, and what might my life had been but for the fact that I would frequently see Brother Phillips riding up the road, and always would make up my mind that I would rather have the kind of religion he had than to own the world. It was Jesus who said to his disciples, 'Ye are the salt of the earth.' Blessed is the circuit rider that can ride up the country road and convict plowboys, three or four hundred yards in the cornfield on either side of the road, without knowing they are even there."

On the glorious night Buddy was saved, he could possess no possible insight nor understanding of the marvelous things he would be led to do in his work for the Lord. The young boy galloped home, filled with the Holy Spirit, a great joy, and a never ending song of praise for his Savior who made him a new creature, and a precious child of God. Buddy knew at last, he was an orphan no more.

What a dear Savior, what a precious salvation, what a glorious life, and what a wonderful story, the story of our own beloved, Reverend Henry Clay Morrison.

The End

Part II
Facts, Comments and Accolades Concerning the Influential Life of Henry Clay Morrison

• Henry Clay Morrison was born in Bedford, Trimble County, Kentucky, March 10, 1857 and died March 24, 1942.

• "For more than sixty years, he crossed the American continent, wielding the sword of the Spirit as only a God anointed man can do. There have been few men his equal as a preacher, his graceful manner, his personal appearance, his eloquent speech and the anointing of the Spirit all combined to make him a mighty man of God in his generation. Kentucky Methodism has probably never produced his equal." (Dr. William L. Clark)

• Morrison established in 1888, the *Pentecostal Herald*, a religious newspaper, (first titled *The Old Methodist* and *The Kentucky Methodist*), and was the editor for 54 years. He noted, "I was divinely called to establish a paper in order to send out an evangelistic message to fields where it was impossible for me to go, personally." The *Pentecostal Herald* was the lifeline of Asbury College and the Asbury Theological Seminary. Morrison said in 1934, 85 to 90 percent of its money has come from the readers of the *Herald*. During his lifetime, nearly 65 million copies were distributed. At its peak, a weekly circulation of 55,000 copies were mailed out to at least 46 states, the District of Columbia and 566 copies to foreign countries.

• Morrison's Pentecostal Publishing Company printed approximately 5 million books and pamphlets, with the distribution of these books being in the multiple millions. Through its bookstore in Louisville, Kentucky, it sold an average of more than $50,000 worth of bibles each year, thus making it one of the twelve largest distributors of bibles in America.

• Morrison was a popular author, having written at least 25 books. Several of these sold as many as 75,000 copies. One went through eight editions in six months. Some have been translated into different languages, especially Japanese and Chinese. Most of his books have been reprinted and are still available today.

• Morrison served as President of Asbury College from 1910-1925, and again from 1933-1940. On both occasions Morrison took on the position to save the school from financial ruin.

• In 1923, Morrison founded the Asbury Theological Seminary, and continued as its president until his death in 1942.

• "From the time Morrison received his first license to preach in the summer of 1878, there was not a year that he was not actively engaged in preaching. Throughout his life, he conducted evangelistic campaigns in at least 40 states, and 13 other countries. In America, Morrison's meetings included large churches as well as small ones. His itinerary included practically all the large cities in the United States. It is estimated that Morrison held at least 1200 revivals, preached not less than 15,000 times, traveled over 500,000 miles and saw more than 30,000 people converted, during his 63 years of ministry." (Percival A. Wesche)

• Morrison was also a well-known camp-meeting preacher. He preached in approximately 250 such campaigns. Since these services occupied his time for nearly three months every summer, a total of nearly 12 years of Morrison's life was spent away from home, preaching and living in these camp meeting sites. Many of the camps were very primitive and offered little in the way of comfort and pleasing accommodations. Although some camp meetings were nice, Morrison often spent two weeks living in a small tent, with a dirt floor and a 2 x 4 with a nail in it for a place to hang his clothes and hat.

• Morrison has been credited as being one of the most important leaders of the Holiness Movement.

• *Christian Century Magazine* in 1924, numbered Henry Clay Morrison among the top 25 preachers in America.

• "One of the great personalities of American Methodism during the past 50 years has been Dr. Henry Clay Morrison. As an eloquent preacher of the gospel, with power to grip and to hold the masses, he has few equals. Recently, at the New Jersey Annual Conference, he packed a great auditorium every day for a week. He was never sensational, but he made the gospel an amazing sensation. His sermons were unforgettable." (Editor of the *New York Christian Advocate*, 1938)

• "To him was given by nature, and nature's God a heart to move the multitude, a mind to think God's thoughts, a voice to rouse his century, his church, and his country. Dr. Morrison was endowed with the prophet's vision and fire; the warrior's courage and daring, and the passion of the soul winner." (George W. Ridout)

• "One of the great men of the religious life of America has passed from us, the last of the old Southern orators. There will never be another Southern orator like him, I suppose. It was in his blood, in his frame, in his make-up. When he fell at last there was a great vacancy upon the horizon, as if a great oak tree had gone and left a vacancy." (E. Stanley Jones)

• "Dr. Morrison is one of the ablest preachers in this country. He is logical and evangelical." (Bishop Charles McCabe)

• "I regard Dr. Morrison as the ablest expounder of the doctrine of the Holy Spirit on the American continent today." (Bishop Willard Mallalieu)

• "I regard Henry Clay Morrison the greatest pulpit orator on the American Continent." (Nebraska Senator and three time Presidential Candidate, William Jennings Bryan)

Publications by
Henry Clay Morrison

Henry Clay (H.C.) Morrison was the author of over 25 books and religious publications including:

- *Answer's Inside (Five Great Needs)* – 1930
- *Baptism with the Holy Ghost* – 1900
- *Battle of the Ballots* – 1928
- *Christ of the Gospels* – 1926
- *Commencement Sermons (Delivered in Asbury College Chapel)* – 1915
- *Confessions of a Backslider* – 1930
- *Crossing the Dead Line / The Re-crucifixion of the Lord Jesus Christ* – 1924
- *Dr. Star and the White Temple* – ca. 1899
- *First Ten Thousand Years in Hell* – 1920 (Essays by various students; forward by Morrison)
- *Follies of Fosdick* – 1936
- *From Sinai to Calvary* – 1942
- *From the Pulpit to Perdition* – 1899
- *Is the World Growing Better or is the World Growing Worse* – 1932
- *Life Sketches and Sermons* – 1903
- *Open Letters to the Church: Bishops, Ministers and Members of the Methodist Episcopal Church, South* – 1910
- *Optimism of Premillennialism* – 1927

- *Pearl of Greatest Price* – 1910s
- *Pentecostal Songs (with Prof. George E. Kersey and John McPherson) songbook* – 1900
- *Presence of God* – 1920s
- *Prophecies Fulfilled and Fulfilling (Lectures on Prophecy)* – 1915
- *Remarkable Conversions, Interesting Incidents and Striking Illustrations* – 1925
- *Romanism and Ruin* – 1914
- *Second Coming of Christ* – 1914
- *Sermons for the Times* – 1921
- *Some Chapters of My Life Story* – 1941
- *Thoughts for the Thoughtful* – 1912
- *The Two Lawyers* – 1898
- *What Think Ye of Christ? Whose Son is He?* – 1920s
- *Will God Set Up A Visible Kingdom On Earth?* – 1934
- *Will A Man Rob God?* – 1920s
- *World Tour of Evangelism* – 1911
- *World War in Prophecy* – 1917

Morrison also wrote innumerable sermons and editorials on religious matters in his own publication, the *Pentecostal Herald*, covering a span of 54 years.

South Central Kentucky Places of Interest in the Life of Henry Clay Morrison

• **William B. Morrison home** where Henry Clay Morrison was raised, his boyhood home.

• **Boyd's Creek Methodist Church** – A third Boyd's Creek church now stands on Siloam Road very near the spot where Morrison attended and was converted in December 1871. A monument stands on the lawn of the church commemorating Morrison's life and conversion here.

The boyhood home of Henry Clay Morrison. The home was located on Hwy 63 across the road from Morrison Park Camp-Meeting grounds, and a few hundred yards north, toward Glasgow. (Photo courtesy of Asbury Theological Seminary.)

• **Boyd's Creek** – The creek where Morrison played, hunted and roamed as a boy. He was baptized here after his conversion.

• **John O. Morrison Home** – The location is off Highway 63 to the right, just past Boyd's Creek, heading toward Morrison Park. John Organ Morrison came to Barren County from Fauquier County, Virginia in 1793. Often referred to as Captain Morrison, he acquired about one hundred acres of land, which included the property where Henry Clay was raised and the grounds where the Camp Meeting now stands. John O. Morrison built the first brick home in the community. According to a December 5th, 1954 *Courier Journal Magazine* article, the home of John O. Morrison was a regular lodging place for the first Bishop of the Methodist Church in America, Francis Asbury. When Morrison died in 1841, the house was acquired through inheritance by his daughter, Mary Jane. Mary Jane married Peter Emory Hammer, raising their family in this home. As years went by, the home became more commonly known as the Hammer House, and the great hill rising above it, was known as Hammer Hill. John O. Morrison, his two wives, and many family relatives are buried in the nearby Morrison-Hammer Cemetery.

What happened in later years to the home would have been a source of great sadness to H.C. Morrison. In the mid to late 1950s, for safety's sake, the state highway department decided to by-pass this section of the road where the old brick home stood. The great hill that lay beyond the home was considered very dangerous and treacherous. Newspaper accounts of the time describe many serious accidents on this hill, and pleas were made for the road to be changed or straightened. When the new section of Highway 63 was completed, the old Morrison home and cemetery was by-passed and left alone to itself. In January 1965, the last descendent to occupy the home, Emory Hammer, passed away. Now the home remained empty, with the only living relative, his sister, Helen Hammer, living far away in New York City. The house was soon vandalized. Someone broke into the home, virtually destroying it along with all its contents. People of the community wandered by pilfering through its remains. The old deserted house and the neglected cemetery became notorious for many a fantastic ghost story. Some told tales of a ghostly misty figure that many claim to have seen.

The house remained in this condition for several years, finally meeting its end on Halloween night in 1969, when the structure was set ablaze by an arsonist. A year or two later an old barn that stood near the cemetery was also destroyed by fire. The house was later bulldozed into a pile of rubble and that is how it remains to this day.

The John O. Morrison Home, (Hammer House) as it appeared in the 1960s. (Photo courtesy of Stephen D. Morrison, Doraville, Georgia.)

• **Morrison-Hammer Cemetery** – The cemetery is a few hundred feet away from where the John O. Morrison house once stood. The cemetery has been neglected over the years, even though some efforts have been made for its benefit. A chain link fence was put around the cemetery for protection, and it has been cleaned and cleared on several occasions. Those buried here include: John O. Morrison, August 10, 1771 - October 15, 1841; John's two wives, Margaret B. Morrison, July 4, 1776 - March 1, 1813 and Elizabeth Morrison, November 8, 1791 - September 12, 1863. Also buried here is Lizzie Morrison, the wonderful aunt who cared for young Henry Clay. The marker gives her date of death as May 15, 1890, and reports her age to be 77 years and 9 months. Peter Emory Hammer, who encouraged young Henry Clay at the mourner's bench, and his wife, Mary Jane Morrison, are buried here, along with many other members of the Hammer family. Other surnames include: Watson, Glass, Barlow, Dotson, Harris, Eaton, Taylor and, of course, Morrison. It seems quite certain that Henry Clay's grandparents, William B. and Frances (Scott) Morrison, are buried here, but no stone has been found for either of them. One researcher lists forty-one known people buried here.

Two children of Henry Clay Morrison, Helen and Frank, visit the Morrison-Hammer Cemetery in the 1960s. (Photo courtesy of Stephen D. Morrison, Doraville, Georgia.)

• **Morrison Retirement Home in Glasgow** – "After having seen the beautiful log house that his friend, Rev. J.L. Piercy (Methodist minister from Glasgow, Kentucky) built on what is now the 31-E Bypass just outside of town, Morrison decided he would build a log home also. Morrison was planning to retire in Glasgow, so he purchased a wooded tract of two and a half acres on what is now North Race Street. Construction started in early 1937 and continued in a spasmodic manner until November 1938. In the intervals between his revival duties, Morrison made more than twenty trips to

Newspaper advertisement from 1942 showing Morrison's retirement home in Glasgow, Kentucky.

Glasgow to check on the progress that was being made. The finished product was a two-story log home, which sat a good distance from the road with many fine shade trees. The seven-room house had four bedrooms, each with its own fireplace and private bath. In addition to the house, the property included a large two and a half-story garage. Morrison's dream of retirement and rest never materialized." According to author Percival A. Wesche, who studied Morrison's diaries, he reports that "Morrison actually spent less than two weeks in his Glasgow home. Furniture was placed in the house on July 13, 1938, and Morrison stayed there until July 19. Two of his daughters, Anna Laura Young and Helen Morrison, spent the weekend with him there, the largest family gathering to stay in the house. He did not return until June 9, 1939, when he spent one night and reported having had 'a good rest.' A week later he came back, but only for a few hours, since he had to move on to Scottsville, Kentucky where he was helping Rev. Piercy in a revival service. One year later, Morrison and his daughter, Anna Laura, spent four days in Glasgow, June 18-21. During this time, he wrote several chapters for his book, *Some Chapters of My Life Story*, as well as several sermons. Aside from two more brief visits of only a few hours each, during which he was arranging for the care of the property, he never visited the house again."

A newspaper advertisement from 1942 shows the Morrison home. The home still stands at 1002 North Race Street beside the Glasgow Christian Church. The outside has been covered with vinyl, but is still recognizable. According to J.L. Piercy, the house cost no less than $10,000 to build. Morrison had deeded the property to his daughters. After Morrison's death in 1942, the house sold at auction in order to settle the estate. It brought only $7,600. (From *Henry Clay Morrison 'Crusader Saint'* by Percival A. Wesche.)

• **Morrison Park Community and the Holiness Camp Meeting** – In 1900, Morrison returned to his boyhood home to conduct the first of what would become an annual revival, and the development of a camp meeting site. Who prompted this first meeting is unknown, but the local paper recorded that it was something Morrison had planned to do for quite some time. A *Courier Journal* article of July 5, 1911, notes that a wealthy Barren County farmer, B.K. Nuckols, was one of the instigators of the plan to build the park.

The annual camp meetings usually lasted for a two-week period. The first meetings were held under a large tent on the very ground where Morrison worked and lived as a boy. Some camped on the grounds, while others came and went. It was so successful that Morrison promised to return the next year. Through the years, the camp meeting progressed and expanded. By 1913, a large open-air wooden tabernacle was constructed, along with several cottages, and even a nice kitchen and dining area was provided for those who stayed on the grounds. The evangelist that year, W.P. Yarbrough of Leesville, South Carolina, wrote that on the last Sunday of the meeting, there was over one thousand in attendance. The meetings were a very popular event and flourished for years. There were many notable evangelists, speakers and singers who came to the park. Two of the most prominent national personalities were World War 1 hero, Alvin C. York (1935) and RCA Victor recording artist, Tony Fontaine (1968 and 1969).

Although Morrison was in much demand for services all around the country, he returned whenever he could. In the 42 years he lived after the park was established, Morrison returned to the camp meeting at least 15 times: 1900, 1903, 1904, 1907, 1908, 1917, 1930, 1931, 1932, 1933, 1934, 1935, 1936, 1937 and 1939.

The park was originally called "Pentecostal Park," a name that Morrison himself chose. By the mid-1930s, the entire area soon became more commonly known as Morrison Park. As time went on, Morrison provided land for a new building to replace the aging "Bald Knob" School that Morrison had attended as a young boy. The new school, called "Morrison Park," was known to have been constructed as early as 1910. It was a more modern one-room facility built just down the road from the camp meeting. Later, Josh Barbour built and operated a little grocery there and a lot of families living nearby created the Morrison Park community.

In June and July 1931, Morrison spent a great amount of time at the site, spending his own money to enlarge the tabernacle, building a workers' cottage, and providing for other improvements to the park and grounds.

In 1934, Morrison sponsored the building of a log structure, 40 x 20 feet, to house a library of Holiness books, and to be used as a small auditorium for committee meetings and prayer services. This restored building stands today and is named in honor of Morrison as the Morrison Library cabin.

Morrison loved his old home place and all the wonderful people he knew and grew up with and never forgot them. In a letter he wrote to a friend, Morrison said, "Whoever has wet their feet, or whoever has had relatives that have wet their feet in Boyd's Creek, Barren County, Kentucky, I claim as my kinfolks."

In 1911, Morrison was asked to lay the cornerstone for the new Methodist church being built on South Green Street in Glasgow.

Painting by Gary Bewley depicting Rev. H.C. Morrison around 1900 when he established the camp meeting in Barren County.

Morrison Visits His Birthplace

In May of 1937, eighty-year-old Morrison, accompanied by his daughter, Helen, came back to Bedford, Kentucky to visit the old house where he was born. An article in the *Trimble Democrat* newspaper (June 3, 1937) recorded this account.

Dr. H.C. Morrison and His Daughter Visit Birthplace

"About ten days ago, Dr. H.C. Morrison of Louisville, a most eminent minister of the Southern Methodist Church, editor of the "Pentecostal Herald" and President of Wilmore College, in company with his daughter, Helen, came to Bedford to visit his birthplace, now owned by Mr. and Mrs. C.M. Cutshaw and daughters. He entered the dining room, the room in which he was born, and turned to Helen and said, "Helen, in here, right over in that corner, is the place your father first saw the light. When I was a few weeks old my mother left me in here in the care of a Mrs. Morgan while she went to Hickory Grove church. When she returned she picked me up in her arms and danced around the room shouting, "I gave my little Henry to the Lord today to preach the gospel, and I believe He accepted my gift." She has been gone many years and here I am the answer to her prayer."

He then asked to see the big living room of which he had heard his grandmother speak. As he entered that room he remarked that it was large enough to hold a protracted meeting. Before leaving the house, he offered a prayer for the happiness and material success for those living within the sacred walls of the old home, for the people of Bedford and of Trimble County, Kentucky. He then hurried on his way, pausing only long enough to pay tribute to an old rock in the front yard and a few of the old trees and vines which have been there so long. Dr. Morrison was eighty years old on March 10, 1937, and is still preaching the gospel, both in the pulpit and over the radio."

Birthplace of Henry Clay Morrison, Bedford, Kentucky, ca. 1921.

NOTE: It was with much effort, and with the kind assistance of Bedford attorney Bobby True, that the actual location of the birthplace house was discovered. The house is no longer standing. A newer brick home stands on the spot at the address of 265 Cutshaw Lane, just off Highway 421 North, near downtown Bedford, Kentucky.

First Camp Meeting at Morrison Park

Taken from Newspaper Accounts, 1900

June 15th - The tent meeting to be held at the Morrison old homestead four miles from town on the Temple Hill road begins Friday evening next, June 22nd at half past seven o'clock. A large tent has been secured and will be put up. Everything possible will be done for the comfort and convenience for those attending the services. The meeting will be conducted by Rev. H. C. Morrison, the noted evangelist. Mr. Morrison is a native of Barren County and it is at his home place that the meeting is to be held. It has been the intention for several years to return to his old home and hold just such a meeting as is contemplated but the pressing demands upon his time has prevented him from doing so until now. He needs no introduction to our people. He is known to them as a brilliant man and an able, eloquent preacher, and one of the grandest meetings in the history of the county is predicted. It is already being discussed in all parts of the country and tremendous crowds are expected to attend.

June 26th - The camp meeting on the Morrison farm near town, commenced last Friday and fairly large crowds are being attracted, though the rains that have fallen since it commenced greatly interfere with the attendance. Rev. H. C. Morrison, who is conducting the meeting, preaches with his old time vigor and earnestness. With favorable weather this week, the attendance promises to be immense and great results are looked for.

HEAR!

Dr. H. C. MORRISON
At Pentecostal Park
SUNDAY, 3 p. m., SEPTEMBER 7th.
Great enterprise on hand. Be sure to COME.

A broadside from 1931 announcing Dr. Morrison will be speaking at Morrison Park. At this time the park was still often referred to as Pentecostal Park. (Photo courtesy of Carl Davis.)

July 2nd – The Morrison Park meeting closed Sunday night. It was one of the greatest meetings held in the county. Notwithstanding the unfavorable weather which continued throughout the entire time, large congregations greeted every service. The crowd Sunday was one of the largest ever assembled at a religious service in this section. There were about 60 conversions during the meeting and the greatest awakening of religious interest ever known in that section.

July 6th – The Camp Meeting on Morrison Park (July 2nd) ended today and the Rev. H. C. Morrison left for his home near Anchorage, KY. The meeting was a success from start to finish. At every service, large and attentive congregations assembled and great interest was manifested at all times. The sermons were delivered with logic, force and eloquence. The singing was conducted in an able manner by Professor Kersey. Brother Morrison left under a promise of returning sometime next summer or fall and holding another meeting. One great source of pleasure to him was the meeting with many of his relatives and friends of his youth and spending the time on the ground over which he had worked in childhood and youth and drinking water from one of the best and purest fountains in the country. (All from the *Glasgow Republican*).

This 2018 painting by Gary Bewley shows Morrison at Morrison Park, as he appeared about 1909. He is standing front and center. The other evangelists depicted (and noting at least one of the years they were at the park) are front row, left to right: Evangelist J.B. Kendall (1906), Rev. C.E. Roberts (1908), Rev. George Floyd Taylor (1909), Bro. Andrew Johnson (1921), Rev. C.P. Gossett (1921), Morrison (standing), Rev. J.L. Piercy, of Glasgow (preached and assisted many times, featured evangelist as early as 1916), Beck Brothers, A.S. Beck and R.S. Beck (1931, 32), Rev. B.G. Carnes (1933). Back row, left to right: Rev. E.A. Ferguson (1905), Rev. W.P. Yarbrough of Leesville, South Carolina (1913), Rev. John Robert Marrs of Mansville, Kentucky (1917), Bro. C.F. Wimberley (1919), Rev. J.R. Parker (1938), Rev. Ernest Dixon, partially seen, (1940), Morrison (center) Rev. Henry W. Blackburn, mostly hidden (1964), Bishop U.V. W. Darlington (1935), Rev. Kenton H. Bird of Wilmore, Kentucky (1922), Dr. Jordon Witt Carder of Wilmore (1915), Rev. Virgil Moore from Asbury College (1937), Rev. L.E. Squires from Fountain Run, Kentucky (1918).

A young Henry Clay Morrison photographed in Glasgow, Kentucky by local photographer, Adolph Rapp, ca. 1896. (Photo courtesy of Asbury Theological Seminary.)

The Bald Knob School near Morrison Park pictured in 1899. Morrison wrote that he and his sister Emma attended this school.

MY FAVORITE PHOTO -- This photo shows the school and student body of Morrison Park School on December 13, 1910. The teacher was Miss Nora Mansfield. First row, left to right, are Mallie Lee Harlow, Zora Harlow, Jimmy Ray Nuchols, Harry Dee Button, H.C. Mayor, Valiera Harlow. Second row, Paul Harlow, Taylor Harlow, Carlos Nuckols, Hub Bailey, Brent Mayor, Myrtie Slayton, Lillie Nuckols, Jewell Mayor, Verda Harlow, Virginia Harlow, Geneva Matthews, Mary Paul Mayor, Ollie Mayor and Myrtie Nuckols. Third row, Millie Slayton, Rosie Bailey, Lou Bailey, Allie Slayton, Emma Mayor, Dovie Mayor, Nevie Matthews, Pearl Button, Lillian Mayor and Ethel Nuckols.

*Morrison Park School group, November 5, 1910. (**Note:** The Mayor names are a misprint; the name is Mayo.)*

MY FAVORITE PHOTO -- This photo, a favorite of Lena Barlow, Glasgow, shows the Morrison Park School class of 1914. First row, left to right, are Nina Barbour, - - Oliver, Tommy Ruth Nuckols, Elliot Matthews, Bertha Mayor, Euke Oliver, Delmer Oliver, Evelyn Bailey, Mollie Bailey, Clotiel Harlow. Second row, Pertie Nuckols, Pauline Matthews, Mollie Harlow, Ruby Nuckols, Herbie Stout, Paul Sabens, Floyd Nuckols, George Oliver, Gus Nuckols, Eulis Mayor, Morris Matthews, Elzie Matthews, Pauline Travis. Third row, Cecil Matthews, Paul Bailey, Lottie Matthews, Valiera Harlow, Lenora Stout, Mae Oliver, Blondell Nuckols, Zora Harlow, Allen Nuckols, H.C. Mayor, Haskell Sabens, Harry B. Barton, Russell Bailey, Glenn Travis, Horace Travis, Paul Harlow, May Bailey, Mary Paul Mayor, Maude Bailey, Myrtle Slayton, Dovie Mayor, Jo Ann Barbour, Nevie Matthews. Fifth row, Taylor Harlow, Link Barbour and Carlos Nuckols. The teacher was Miss Elizabeth Edwards.

*Morrison Park School, 1914 (**Note**: The Mayor names are a misprint; the name is Mayo.)*

Boyd's Creek School, ca. 1910. Teacher Fleming C. Underwood is pictured in the center.

Morrison Park School group, November 15, 1915.

Morrison Park School 1937. Top row: Margaret Matthews, Sarah Marshall, Elsie Wells, Second row: George Smith, Paul Luster, Flossie Grace, Lucille Troxall, J.C. Bowles, John Harlin, Edna Underwood, [William Floyd] or George Troxall, Lula Grace, Leeson Burgess, Third row: Mary Lou Strode, Barbara Moore, Jean Stewart, Frances Wells, Lougene Troxall, Robert Luster, Lee Raymond Bewley, Paul Piercy. Bottom row; Haiden T. McGuire, Johnny Burgess, James Smith, Virginia Bewley, Maxine Bewley, Pauline Matthews, Genese Pedigo, teacher, Elizabeth Pedigo.

A group gathered for a photo at Morrison Park in the mid-1940s. Seated from left: Dora Harwood, Rev. Freeman V. Harwood, Bessie Andrews and Rev. S.F. Andrews, Rev. J.L. Piercy, and Joe Andrews (son of Mr. and Mrs. S.F. Andrews.) Joe became a minister and later conducted services here with his father in the 1960s. The people in the back row are unidentified.

A service in the 1970s inside the tabernacle.

An early photo of the tabernacle and grounds at Morrison Park. (Photo courtesy of Bill Hewitt, from the collection of Gilbert and Lily (Rogers) Hewitt.)

A photo of the Park ca. 1970. (Photo courtesy of South Central Kentucky Cultural Center.)

The park and tabernacle looking from Highway 63.

Part III
The Restoration of Morrison Park

The Morrison Park Camp Meeting took place each year until the late 1990s, when deterioration of the park along with storm damage, caused the tabernacle to be torn down. The last services were held in tents as it had started. However, the lack of support and reduction in attendance caused the nearly one hundred year old event to cease.

The Morrison Park campground sat unused and neglected for at least eleven years and most everyone feared the last remnants of the park would be lost forever. (Photographs courtesy of W. S. Everett.)

In December 2010, a group of concerned citizens began restoration of the park. The condition was deplorable. The cabins were in great disrepair. The library cabin had been overrun with squirrels, birds and filled with junk. The smaller J.L. Piercy cabin was partially on the ground with rotten logs and floor. The grounds were overgrown with weeds, trees and briars, and were virtually impassible.

After a hard day's work, Nancy Richey (WKU) shows one of the massive piles of growth she helped cut from the grounds.

Buck Riddle, Gary Bewley and Delbert Birge (right) stop for a moment to be photographed as they restore the Rev. J.L. Piercy cabin.

Buck Riddle, who has been in construction all his life, had the experience and ability to restore the old cabin, which was almost beyond repair.

The clearing of the park has taken years, and it still continues. The cabin required a new roof, new floor and several logs to be replaced. The work on the cabin began in October 2011 and took several months to complete. Bob Bell also assisted with the project. No one took any money for their hard work. It was a labor of love for the park, and for the Lord.

New footing for the Rev. J.L. Piercy Cabin.

Buck Riddle makes a log fit into place, as Bob Bell (background) assists.

Mike Hudspeth, (left) is pictured with the new Morrison Park sign he designed, built and donated to the park. Wonderful giving people like Mike have enabled the park to be restored. Gary Bewley stands beside Mike and Buck Riddle (right).

In May 2014, a group of people gather for the dedication of a new Kentucky Historical Marker. The marker honors Henry Clay Morrison and the park he founded here in 1900. Many of Morrison's great-grandchildren attended this event.

The placement of the Kentucky Historical Marker at Morrison Park was important in honoring the park and Morrison's great contribution in the history of American religion. Sandi Gorin, President of the Barren County Historical Society and its members paid and provided placement for this marker. This is another great example of community support for the preservation of Morrison Park.

Henry Clay Morrison's great-grandchildren came from all parts of the country to attend the dedication ceremony for the Kentucky Historical Marker. Seated from left: Debra Hoffman and Elizabeth Hoffman Ross. Standing from left: Joseph Hoffman, George Hoffman, Mike Ross, and Nelson Hoffman.

Rev. Timothy Shirley (in front with Bible) conducted the first service at the park since the restoration began. Since that time, there have been several other services and weddings held in the Morrison Memorial Library Cabin. (Photo courtesy of Harold Kelley.)

The Library cabin was built by Morrison to house religious and Holiness books, and to serve as a place to assemble for conferences and prayer meetings. The cabin has been renovated to a chapel type atmosphere and the second level features a Morrison museum.(Photo courtesy of Harvey Simmons.)

Edie Bell, along with her husband Bob, are neighbors to the park, and have worked tirelessly to turn the grounds into something spectacular. Many people visit the park throughout the year just to see the beautiful flowers and landscape.

A map of the Morrison Park area is pictured on the opposite page. The "Bald Knob" school was remodeled and converted into a house that still stands on Bristletown Road. The Bailey Cemetery contains the graves of many who lived in Morrison Park. The Morrison Park School and the William Morrison cabin, where Morrison grew up, have been gone for many years; the map indicates where they stood. Hwy. 63 has been altered over the years, mostly straightening out bad hills and curves. The old road where the Morrison/ Hammer Cemetery and John O. Morrison Home are located are part of the old road. It was changed in the late 1950s. In the early 1990s, the state highway department cut a great gap out of the Morrison Park hill and straightened a winding curve over the hill from the park.

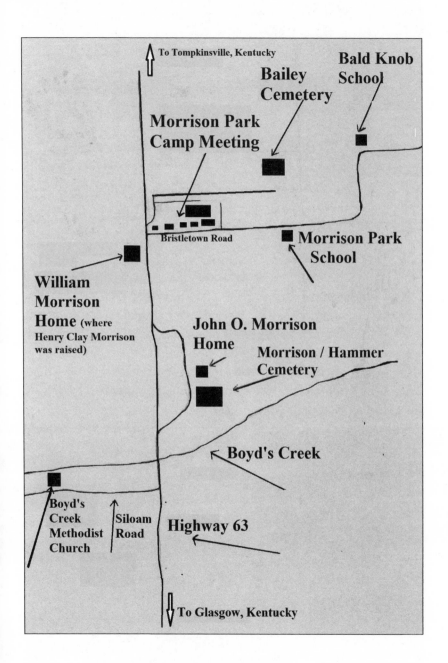

To Tompkinsville, Kentucky

Bald Knob School

Bailey Cemetery

Morrison Park Camp Meeting

Bristletown Road

Morrison Park School

William Morrison Home (where Henry Clay Morrison was raised)

John O. Morrison Home

Morrison / Hammer Cemetery

Boyd's Creek

Boyd's Creek Methodist Church

Siloam Road

Highway 63

To Glasgow, Kentucky

A fundraising effort began in 2015 to garner funding for a new tabernacle. Donations were received from churches, organizations and individuals. The tabernacle was named in honor of Carl Jackson, a dedicated supporter of our restoration efforts. The original trusses, seen at center, were used in the rebuilding. The new structure, at its original site, was completed in the summer of 2016 by Two Brothers Construction.

The dedication of the tabernacle on September 11, 2016.

Harold Kelley 2017

With the completion of the tabernacle, the park has now been fully restored for public use. The restroom building, small cabins and the J.L. Piercy cabin (above) and the Morrison Library cabin (below), are results of the efforts of the community. (Photos courtesy of Harold Kelley.)

Other Barren County, Kentucky monuments dedicated to Henry Clay Morrison; below left, monument dedicated at Morrison Park Camp Meeting site soon after his death in 1942. Below right, monument at Boyd's Creek Methodist Church, the site of his conversion.

Morrison is also honored in numerous ways at Asbury College at Wilmore, Kentucky and at the Asbury Theological Seminary, which he founded in 1923.

Gary Bewley is pictured at a monument dedicated to Morrison at Indian Springs Holiness Camp Meeting in Flovilla, Georgia, where Morrison preached almost every year.

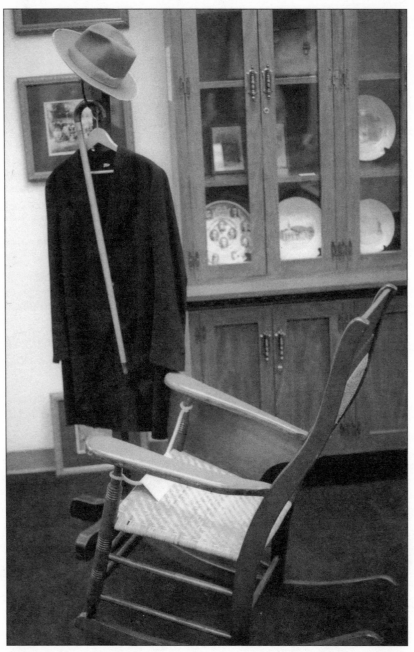

Morrison's hat, coat and rocking chair on display at the library of Asbury College.

Tribute to Reverend James Phillips

"Reverend James Phillips was born in Taylor County, Kentucky, April 27, 1848. He entered the Louisville Conference as a Methodist preacher in 1870 and served in numerous districts in the conference. He married Mrs. Jennie Rankin of Brandenburg, Kentucky, September 30, 1880. They had two daughters. Rev. Phillips died March 26, 1886. A short biography at the time of his death stated, he was not a brilliant preacher, but his success was marvelous. He received during his short ministry, sixteen hundred members! He was a sweet singer, gifted in prayer, a fine pastor and universally loved. He was an all-round man, committing his soul, his family, the church all to God.

Phillips was converted under the ministry of Rev. C.D. Donaldson, and soon after felt he was called to the ministry. He was about twenty-two years old at this time. From his early life he was a cripple, frequently having to use both cane and crutch. His style was very plain and simple, practical and earnest; but by a deep personal experience he knew his doctrine to be of God, and delivered his message assured of its truth. Burdened with the worth of souls, he sought for and expected results. He was a good pastor and a good man, full of faith and of the Holy Ghost. The last illness of Brother Phillips was brief. He had suffered for months because of rheumatic trouble in his disabled hip, but with steady zeal prosecuted his work till ten days before his death. He seemed impressed that the end had come, and while expressing a wish to live for the sake of his family and the church, he was resigned, peaceful, happy, realizing that to 'die is gain.' He sweetly fell asleep at 10 o'clock A.M., March 26, 1884. He was buried in Brandenburg, Kentucky. His Elder, Rev. E.R. Harrison said in his memory, "I knew none more true, more faithful, more efficient than was he."

—*From the Minutes of the Forty-First Session of the Louisville Annual Conference (1886)*

Mary Mae Mayo Bewley (1891-1975)

The family of William D. Mayo, living in the old Morrison Home. Photo ca.1912. Back row from left: Ellis Mayo, Jewell (Mayo) Harvey, Gracie (Mayo) Button, Mary Mae (Mayo) Bewley, and Dovie (Mayo) Stout. Front row from left: Bertha (Mayo) Davis, Amanda (Stout) Mayo, H.C. Mayo, Harry D. Button, William D. Mayo, and daughter Ollie (Mayo) Williams, at right, behind his shoulder.

Tribute to Mary Mae Mayo Bewley

In conclusion, this book is also dedicated to my dear grandmother, Mary Mae Mayo Bewley (1891-1975). My grandmother grew up at Morrison Park and was raised in the very log cabin that H.C. Morrison lived in as a boy. She attended the camp meetings at Morrison Park, and met Henry Clay Morrison there on many occasions. On Sunday mornings, we often gathered around the breakfast table, and looked through my family's large picture box. It contained a photo of Bro. Morrison. My grandmother would hold the picture, and talk about how wonderful and great Morrison was. Then she discussed the great old camp meetings she attended there as a young girl and shared many old family stories about Morrison Park. Her father, William D. Mayo was on the road crew who helped work on, care for and pave Highway 63. He was also a carpenter who built a new home right across from the camp ground, and helped with the construction of the tabernacle, the log cabins, and other structures within the park. Her love for Dr. Morrison and Morrison Park has been the seed that inspired the restoration efforts there. I am thankful for my grandmother, her love and her stories that helped keep the past alive in my heart, and with the help of our Lord, will prevent Morrison Park from ever slipping away again. Please keep Morrison Park forever in your prayers. God bless you all.

—Gary Bewley

Board of Directors for Morrison Park Camp Meeting are left to right, Nancy Richey, Gary Bewley, Robert Carver, Buck Riddle, Bob Bell, Edie Bell and Marshall Bailey; absent are Phillip Pursley and Nell Doris Stewart. (Photo by Harold Kelley)

Morrison Camp Meeting Contributors

Virginia Anderson
Awards, Inc.
Rollin and Shirley Bacon
Joel Bailey
Marshall Bailey
Omar Barbour
Robert and Loretta Barbour
Barren County Historical
  Society
Barren River Rod and Gun
  Club
Bobby Joe and Betty Barrick
Bob and Edie Bell
Bethel Methodist Church
Col. Carroll and Anne Bewley
Bro. Gary Bewley
Delbert and Barbara Birge
Kevin Birge
Tootie Bishop
George and Opel Bowles
Margaret Bowles

William Earl and Nell Bowles
Boyd's Creek Methodist Church
Kristy Brawand
Rev. John Brewer
Elizabeth Bruner
Roy and Joyce Buchanan
Johnny and Tong Bullington
Jerry D. and Peg Burgett
Richard and Carol Carver
Bro. Robert Carver
Ernest Chambers
Richard and Carolyn Chambers
Ada Christy
Floyd and Ruby Cockerham
Bro. Dale and Liz Copas
Betty Coulter
Charles and Helen Crabtree
Joey and Jennifer Crews
Mr. and Mrs. Ronnie
  Cunningham
Dannie R. Daniels

Ed Darst
Bro. Billy Neal Davis
John and Allison Day
Geraldine Dennison
Dennis Devore
Carl Dickerson
Dickerson Lumber Company
Lyman and Sally Dixon
Dover Baptist Church, Etoile
East Main Methodist Church
W. S. Everett
Louise Forsythe
Freedom Warriors
Karyl J. George
Gethsemane Baptist Church
Glasgow Electric Plant Board
Cheryl L. Goddard
Golden Oldies, Temple Hill
County Judge Davie Greer
Stanley and Peggy Greer
Francis Groce
Eugene R. Hack
Jerry Harvey
Thomas and Kathy Hassee
Joseph Hoffman
Nelson M. Hoffman
Virginia Houchens
Houchens Industries
Mike and Joan Hudspeth
Lyon Hutcherson Jr.
Carl and Lou Jackson
Harold and Susan Jackson
James Jackson
Lou Jackson
Steven and Katherine Jackson
Tommy Jackson

Wayne and Doris Jackson
Bryan and Kuristen Jones
Floyd Ray Jones, Falling Timber
  Dairy
Gary and Julia Jones
Martha and Stephen Jones
Harold and Patricia Kelley
James and Elsa Knott
Robert L. Knott
Linda Long
Lowes
Gina Lyon
Mrs. Lemmuel Martin
Barbara Matthews
Harold and Anne Matthews
Linda Bewley Mayberry
Georgeann Lewis McCoy
Roger and Wandaline McCoy
Wandaline McCoy
Sue Lynn and Bob McDaniel
David and Sheila Milam
John Robert Miller
Ralph and Virginia Minard
Pat Moore
Bro. Billy and Mable Moran
Steve Morrison
Tommy Morrison
Timothy Mullins
Harrell and Loretta Murray
Rita Neighbors
New Bethel Missionary Baptist
  Church
New Salem Methodist Church
Walter Norris
Doris Oliver
Marjorie Palmore

Connie Pendleton and the
 Siloam Baptist Church
 Sunday School
Howard Perkins
Mrs. Burl Pitcock
Bruce and Dana Powell
Debbie Powell
Scott Queen, State Farm
 Insurance Company
Willard and Mary Randolph
Gale Renner
Glen Renner Family
Bob and Donna Rich
Bruce and Joyce Richey
James and Olene Richey
Tony Richey and the Temple
 Hill Fire Department
Buck and Pat Riddle
Dillard and Mary Rigsby
Roger and Kathy Lee Ritchey Jr.
Michael J. and Elizabeth Ross
Al Sharber
Timmy and Debbie Sherfey
Bro. Timothy and Michelle
 Shirley
Anthony Shoultz
Jimmy and Helen Siddens
Siloam Baptist Church

Danny Simmons
Capt. James A. Simmons
Patricia Slaughter
Joseph and Beverly Smallwood
Charles David Smith
Jimmy Smith
Square Deal Lumber Company
Nell Doris Stewart
Fendall and Marjorie Strode
Wayne and Becky Strode
Gerald Dean and Patricia Taylor
Temple Hill Baptist Church
Rhonda Thomerson
Maxene Underwood
William and Judy Underwood
Marshall and Mary Wagoner
Tony M. Walter
Alecia Webb-Edgington
Fredrica Weber
Jay P. and Aileen Weber
Bro. Jason Wheeley
Lanny Whitlow
Sidney Williams
Mike and Linda Wood
Woodmen of the World
Joyce and Billy Wray
Sharon D. Zamp

Special Thanks

Special thanks to Chris Walker and Zack Folden and Two Brothers Construction for making and donating the beautiful cross to Morrison Park, and for making many of the benches.

Special thanks to Richard Chambers for donating his time and skill to provide all the electrical service for the tabernacle, and to Kelton Scott for plumbing services.

Special thanks to Becky and Bobby Joe Barrick of Awards Inc. for donating the plates and signs for the benches, and for others who have made special donations.

Special thanks to Buck Riddle for many, many hours of very hard work on most every building and part of our reconstruction. He donated his time, his tools and professional experience to make the restoration happen.

Special thanks to Matt Mutter, Roger Gentry and the Barren County Correctional Center inmates work program for mowing and weed eating the park grounds.

Special thanks to Bob and Edie Bell for all their hard work providing the wonderful flowers that they have planted, the donation of many arts and crafts for Roller Coaster fair, and many other jobs too numerous to mention.

Robert Barbour spent many, many hours clearing, cleaning, painting, and doing much needed work, along with other donations.

Special thanks to the late Delbert Birge for many hours of work on the Piercy Cabin and Restroom building.

Special thanks to Traci Shirley and Terry Houchen for work on the grounds and cabin.

And, a very special thanks to Sandi Gorin and all the members of the Barren County Historical Society, who provided the funds for the Kentucky Highway historical marker honoring Henry Clay Morrison, Ricky Spillman for special help and donation concerning dozer work at the Park, and Tony Clemmons, labor, and various materials (electrical work).

We have had contributions given during services held at the park, along with so many who took part in the fundraising efforts, making, buying, and selling the musical CDs. Special thanks to Wayne Sexton Recording Services, who did so much for us, and to the late Mike Creasy. The performers included:

Dennis Devore, The Greers, Pam Staples, John Shepherd, Wayne Sexton, Marilyn Bunch, Stanley Greet, Joy and Anthony Greer, Phil Patton, Tommie Kay Thomas, Debi Simmons, Sharon Burgess, Susan Russell, Herman Hume, Robbie Jones, The Heavenly Heirs, Randy Richardson, The Edmonton Quartet, Gary Bewley, Susie and Hannah Bryson, Anne Bewley, Shelia Atwell, Kimberly Burgess Hunt, Michelle Burgess Johnson Shirley, Marshall Bailey, and Dane Bowles.

I am quite sure over a nearly nine-year period, we may have left someone out. If we did, it will be the result of a failing memory, not an ungrateful heart.

About the Authors

Gary Bewley is a retired law enforcement officer and minister. A native of Barren County, Kentucky, he grew up and lives within two miles of the boyhood home of Rev. Henry Clay Morrison. Gary serves as president of the Morrison Park Camp-meeting Association and along with Nancy Richey led the restoration efforts at the park. In addition, Gary serves on the board of the Barren County Historical Society, and was pleased to be the initiator for the placement of a local monument honoring musician and Barren County native Billy Vaughn. Gary is also an artist and musician, and spends much time  writing religious material to witness and share the truth of God's word. Although many books have been written by, and about, Henry Clay Morrison, Gary felt there was a special need to emphasize and share with young readers the touching story of Morrison's early life. This illustrated book, along with much local history, he believes, breathes new life into this 160-year-old story, and trusts it will be a great joy and witness to many young people for years to come.

Nancy Richey is an Associate Professor and the Visual Resources Librarian for the Department of Library Special Collections at Western Kentucky University. A native of Mt. Hermon, Kentucky, Richey has been a faculty member at WKU since July 2008. She is a graduate of the University of Kentucky and WKU, where she received degrees in Information Science and Southern History. Richey has served on various historical boards, including Janice Holt Giles Society, Morrison Park Camp Meeting Site Restoration Board and the Daughters of the American Revolution, and has authored/co-authored two local history books in the *Images of America* series

Nancy Richey stands beside the grave of Henry Clay Morrison in the Wilmore, Kentucky city cemetery, near the site of Asbury College and Asbury Theological Seminary.

published by Arcadia Press, as well as a biography, *Mose Roger: Kentucky's Incomparable Guitar Master*, published recently by Acclaim Press. She loves local history and notes that it is not "national history writ small", but that the stories others may have thought "too small" to tell can also be saved in this way.

Index